CAN I TELL YOU ABOUT...?

The 'Can I tell you about...?' series offers simple introductions to a range of conditions, issues and big ideas that affect our lives. Friendly characters invite readers to learn about their experiences, share their knowledge, and teach us to empathise with others. These books serve as excellent starting points for family and classroom discussions.

Other subjects covered in the Can I tell you about...? series

ADHD	Epilepsy
Adoption	Forgiveness
Anxiety	Gender Diversity
Asperger Syndrome	Loneliness
Asthma	ME/Chronic Fatigue
Auditory Processing	Syndrome
Disorder	Multiple Sclerosis
Autism	OCD
Bipolar Disorder	Parkinson's Disease
Cerebral Palsy	Pathological Demand
Compassion	Avoidance Syndrome
Dementia	Peanut Allergy
Depression	Selective Mutism
Diabetes (Type 1)	Self-Harm
Down Syndrome	Sensory Processing
Dyslexia	Difficulties
Dyspraxia	Stammering/Stuttering
Eating Disorders	Stroke
Eczema	Tourette Syndrome

Can I Tell You About...

Gratitude?

A Helpful Introduction for Everyone

Liz Gulliford

Illustrated by Rosy Salaman

Jessica Kingsley *Publishers*
London and Philadelphia

First published in 2018
by Jessica Kingsley Publishers
73 Collier Street
London N1 9BE, UK
and
400 Market Street, Suite 400
Philadelphia, PA 19106, USA

www.jkp.com

Library of Congress Cataloging in Publication Data
A CIP catalog record for this book is available
from the Library of Congress

British Library Cataloguing in Publication Data
A CIP catalogue record for this book is
available from the British Library

ISBN 978 1 78592 457 6
eISBN 978 1 78450 833 3

Printed and bound in Great Britain

MIX
Paper from
responsible sources
FSC
www.fsc.org   FSC® C013056

To Francesca, Edmund, Amelia and Rory.

ACKNOWLEDGEMENTS

I am grateful to my colleagues at the Jubilee Centre for Character and Virtues, based in the School of Education at the University of Birmingham, for their encouragement and support. In particular, my sincere thanks are due to Dr Blaire Morgan and Professor Kristján Kristjánsson with whom I worked on the Centre's Attitude for Gratitude Project from September 2012 to February 2015. This ambitious research project examined how gratitude is understood in the UK, what British people are grateful for and the value people place on this character virtue. The project incorporated a variety of methods to examine these questions, both conceptually and empirically, canvassing the opinions of over 10,000 people in the UK. My involvement in this research played a significant role in refining my understanding of the concept of gratitude – a virtue that is far more complex than is commonly assumed.

CONTENTS

INTRODUCTION

Most of us encounter gratitude on a daily basis. Saying thank you is a normal part of everyday life, which many of us expect as an expression of politeness. But gratitude is more than merely an expression of politeness, and it can be quite complicated. For instance, sometimes we might feel grateful for something someone has done for us or given us, but we feel uncomfortable about it at the same time. Perhaps we know we can't return the favour, or maybe we suspect the motives of the person who benefited us.

For these reasons, gratitude is far from the simple concept many people take it to be. As such, there is a lot to be said for taking a closer look at gratitude. It is especially important for young people to learn about the complexities around gratitude, and for parents, guardians and teachers to promote a discriminate approach when responding to gifts or favours from people in our lives.

The meaning of gratitude is often assumed, rather than directly addressed. Parents and other educators seem to believe that young people will simply pick up what gratitude means and when it is appropriate. Most of us are familiar with the experience of being strongly encouraged – and sometimes even coerced – into saying thank you to be polite. Every time this happens, we reinforce a message about gratitude that might not always be helpful.

It is good to encourage people, young and old, to reflect on gratitude. *Can I tell you about Gratitude?* is a guide for young people aged 7–13, their families, and their teachers and teaching assistants. To make reflection on the meaning of gratitude more engaging, this book weaves considerations about gratitude – what it is, what causes it and when it might and might not be appropriate – into a story about a girl called Maya and her family and friends. *Can I tell you about Gratitude?* has been designed to stimulate discussion about gratitude in the home and in the classroom, giving young people the opportunity to reflect on the complexities of this everyday social emotion and valued strength of character.

"Hello! My name is Maya. I live with my mum, my step-dad, my older brother Arun and my younger sister, who is called Anni. I enjoy being part of a drama club and I'm on the school netball team."

"The week before last it was my birthday. I was given some really great presents and a birthday cake, which Arun made. Mum and Tony, my step-dad, bought me a new bike. It's actually second-hand but it's 'new' to me and, although I hadn't asked them for it, it's exactly what I wanted! I've recently had a growth spurt and they must have noticed that I'd outgrown my old shopper with the bell and tartan shopping basket – its replacement is a mountain bike with 15 gears. I couldn't wait to try it out!

I was really grateful to Mum and Tony for getting me the bike, and I was so delighted I kept on saying 'thank you'. They were pleased to see me so happy! Everyone felt good. I had some other presents too. Dad bought me some new trainers, which are really lovely. I texted him straightaway to say thank you because he would have been at work, and then rang him up again later on when I got back from school to make sure he knew how much I appreciated the gift. I asked him how he knew which ones I wanted but he just said he knows what I like. Well, he *is* my dad!

My brother had saved up his paper round money to buy me a new bike helmet; my head has grown now too, so I needed it. I had other presents and some money from my aunties and uncles. When I got home from school I got in touch with them to say thanks. Nani (that's my mum's mum) bought me a pink scarf. I won't be able to wear *that* on the bike! To be honest, it isn't really my sort of thing – pink isn't my favourite colour and it's got a sparkly silver thread running through it, but I know she meant well when she bought it for me, and she doesn't know I've gone off pink lately.

In any case, not everyone knows *exactly* the right present to get for you. When I was a bit younger I didn't realise this and I was a bit disappointed when people bought me toys I didn't like. I remember being given a doll that you gave a bottle to and then it wet itself. I thought it was horrible! Mum and Dad said it was important to recognise that although people sometimes get the 'wrong' gift for you, their *intention* is to make you happy and you should be grateful for that. As I've grown older, I think I've come to appreciate that it's the thought that counts, but I guess some things take time to realise."

"Having said that, though, I also think it's important to be honest with people – without hurting their feelings – about what sort of things you like. It wouldn't show much thoughtfulness on their part if they kept on getting you things they knew weren't really your cup of tea, but you can't expect other people to read your mind.

I wrote Nani a thank-you note because she likes having letters and photos to stick on her fridge with magnets. It reminds her of us. She lives a long way away and so we don't get to see her very often. It is important to let people know how much you appreciate them and what they do for you. It isn't just a question of politeness – although it is important to remember to say thank you, of course. Mum says it goes deeper than that. It shows that you recognise how much other people give you and that you don't take it for granted.

I agree that gratitude is important. No one likes it when they help people and it goes unnoticed. I suppose people have different ways of showing their gratitude to others – and you have to bear in mind that it matters how old you are as well. Some people show they're grateful simply by saying thank you. Other people might show their appreciation by returning the favour in the future – perhaps not in *exactly* the same way, but to demonstrate some element of reciprocation. I heard that some animals might do that too. Some folks might write a thank-you letter or send a text – you couldn't expect a chimpanzee to do that though!

You have to take someone's age into consideration. I remember when my sister was really little we were helping her to do things all the time – it's just a fact of life for a baby – and until you're a certain age you can't actually say 'thank you', or understand why it might be needed. You have to expect babies to take a lot of things for granted. But when people get older, it's important for them to recognise how much other people do for them. When you stop for a moment and think about how many people are involved in putting a pizza on the table for dinner, you realise just how much all of us rely on other people."

"I remember that last time Nani visited we went for a picnic for Mum's birthday, which is in the summer. Of course, with British weather being what it is, you can never be sure it will be a nice day, no matter what the weather forecast says! Nani prepared a lot of food for the picnic: sandwiches, samosas, salads and dips. We had hot drinks in flasks and cold drinks in a cooler bag. We had to pack everything we needed into the car, which ended up being chock-a-block because we also had to take a blanket, deckchairs and a cricket set! Everyone kept saying they hoped the weather would hold out; we didn't want rain putting out the candles on the birthday cake!

In the end, it was a beautifully sunny
day and something of a debate started about
whether we were lucky, fortunate, glad or
grateful for it. Mum said we'd been lucky, but
Nani said she was *grateful* for such a beautiful
and memorable day. I suppose if you believe
in God (like Nani does) that makes sense. But
if you don't believe in God I guess you couldn't
really say you were grateful to anyone. I know
I felt fortunate, lucky and glad that we'd had
a nice day for the birthday picnic, but I wasn't
sure whether I would say I was grateful. It's a
bit of a puzzle…!"

"I think there's a place for gratitude even when people are just doing their job. A couple of months ago my brother was rushed into hospital with appendicitis. He was in a lot of pain and he was extremely worried about what it was. He had to have an 'emergency appendectomy' – that means he had to have his appendix removed in a hurry! When he came round after the operation we were all so grateful to the surgeon and to all the doctors and nurses who had looked after him. He kept on saying to the surgeon, 'Thank you, you saved my life.' This was absolutely true, of course, but she shrugged it off saying, 'There's no need to say thank you. I was just doing my job.'

I suppose there are a lot of people whose job it is to look after us, one way or another. As well as hospital staff, there are lifeguards and firefighters whose duty it is to take care of us. I don't think that means you don't need to be grateful to them for helping you or rescuing you – if it comes to that. When you think about it, it's our parents' and guardians' duty to take care of us but that doesn't mean there's no need for us to be grateful to them just because it's a part of the 'job description'!

It doesn't have to be a life-threatening situation for us to express our thanks to someone. I suppose when we say thank you to the driver as we step off the bus, or when we thank someone for holding the door open, we do *mean* it, but not in the same way my family did after my brother's emergency operation. I think sometimes gratitude *is* perhaps a question of politeness. We all notice when someone forgets to say thank you, so I reckon it's still a pretty important kind of gratitude."

"I think there are certain things that 'boost' the experience of feeling grateful. A few weeks ago, one of my friends helped me to learn my lines for drama club. He didn't have to go through the script with me – he isn't even in drama club himself – but he knows how important it is for me to be word-perfect in time for our performances. He was very patient going over and over the same section of the play until I got it all right. He didn't have to spend his time doing that, and I certainly didn't expect him to. I was really grateful to him because he went above and beyond what you'd expect of a friend. I mean, you might expect someone to go through it with you once or twice – but he must have listened to me a *lot* more than that! I really appreciated it. I think you feel more grateful when you know people have gone out of their way to help you. It makes you feel valued.

I really love being in drama club. After our last show, there was a sort of competition where we could nominate other people in the cast and crew for an award. There were different categories; some of the awards were for the performers and others were for the people who are involved backstage. I was nominated for my rendition of 'You've got to pick a pocket or two' – I played the Artful Dodger in *Oliver*. It felt really good to be nominated by my companions in the club and I hoped I would win the award. In the end, my friend Steve got more votes than I did. He played Bill Sikes. He had to really *act* that part, though, because he's such a nice guy in real life. In the story, Bill Sikes is a violent and aggressive man who murders his own girlfriend. Steve sang a song where Bill delights in the fact that people are afraid of him. I must say, he did a very good job of playing the villain.

Even though I didn't win the prize, I was still grateful for the nomination and for the votes I received. It's nice to know that people appreciate your performance and want you to win, no matter what the final outcome is. I suppose this is another case where people say, 'It's the thought that counts'. I think there's a lot of truth in that saying, but what about if you're not *sure* what thoughts were really going through someone's head? What if you couldn't be certain of the *intention* they had in giving you something or doing something for you? Let me share with you an example of the sort of thing I mean."

"Last week, something happened at school that left me feeling a bit confused. Laura, who is one of my friends, came back from a weekend away with her family at the seaside. Apparently, they all had a lovely time. Laura said that she'd been thinking about me and, knowing how much I like them, had bought me a pair of dolphin earrings as a gift. She gave me the earrings on Monday and I thought they were beautiful – a really thoughtful present. I've always been fascinated by dolphins and whales.

I thanked Laura very much for the present
– it wasn't even my birthday or anything
so it seemed especially kind of her to have
bought them with her own pocket money and
to have thought of me while she was away.
The earrings were studs, so I was able to wear
them to school, and I could see that Laura was
pleased to see how delighted I was with the
gift. We sat together at lunchtime all week and
made plans to go for a bike ride together at the
weekend.

I wrote Laura a thank-you card because although I'd thanked her face to face, I wanted it to be special. But then it got complicated and I decided not to send the card. I don't feel the same about the earrings now as I did before. I mean, I *love* the earrings – and Laura knows that she couldn't have picked a better present for me. But on Thursday she asked me to give her my history project on the Romans which is due in on Monday. She knows that I spent a lot of time on this homework while she was away last weekend."

"I really like the earrings and I was grateful to Laura for the present. It felt good to know that she was thinking of me. Her kindness also seemed to bring us closer together and I liked spending time with her over lunch. But I am not sure I *should* be grateful any more. It seems to me that she might well have been thinking about me – but not perhaps in the way I thought…!

When Laura asked to borrow my history project I didn't want to say no because she had bought me the earrings and we had enjoyed each other's company so much over the past few days. Then I started to think about *why* she had given me the earrings – what her *motives* had been – and I started to look at it differently. I told her that I wouldn't give her my project. I was shocked she had asked to copy my work. What really upset me, though, was that it seemed she had only given me the earrings to soften me up so that I would do what she wanted. It didn't feel good.

Laura was upset when I refused to loan her my homework and said she didn't want to go for the bike ride with me, which made me feel even worse. I told Tony, my step-dad, what had happened. He said he completely understood how I felt. He said that sometimes people give you things when they have 'an ulterior motive' in mind. In other words, people aren't giving you something or doing something for *you*, they have other, often selfish, aims in mind. In this case, it looked suspiciously like Laura had the goal of borrowing my project on the Romans, which was why I no longer felt as much gratitude to Laura for the earrings as I did at first. In fact, I wasn't sure I felt grateful at all any more. Tony pointed out that you can't always tell what someone's motives are. However, over time and as you get to see how people behave, it tends to become clearer."

"I feel I have learned something from this episode. I realised that we don't always have to be grateful for favours or gifts from other people. It is important to consider whether we have good *reasons* to feel grateful to someone. If someone had what Tony called 'an ulterior motive' in doing us a favour or giving us a gift, then we might have to reconsider whether our gratitude is really called for. It would also be normal to feel mixed emotions. On the one hand, you might feel happy to have been given the lovely earrings. On the other, you could feel upset and disappointed that the gift or favour wasn't *entirely* for your benefit. It can all get rather complicated...

Another way we can experience mixed feelings about gratitude has to do with timing. Sometimes we only feel grateful for something after a certain amount of time has gone by. Our feelings can change, and we can come to be grateful for something that was difficult, uncomfortable or painful at the time. At the end of the Christmas term we had a maths test in which I did very poorly. I only got seven out of twenty questions right and I felt really bad about it as I knew I could have done a whole lot better.

The truth was that I had let myself down because I hadn't put enough time into revising for the test. I thought I would be able to do alright without putting in much effort, but I was proved wrong. Now, I don't think anyone exactly *welcomes* finding that sort of thing out – at least not at first! However, now I'm glad it happened, because since then I've realised that you have to prepare for tests, even if it is in a subject you're good at – like maths. So that was something good that came out of the experience. If you don't make mistakes you can't *learn* from your mistakes – and that is something for which you can, in the end, be grateful.

I think Laura made a mistake with the earrings. I reckon the best course of action is to tell her how I feel about it. I do really like the gift, but she needs to do her own project and, in the end, I'm sure she'll feel much better about doing it herself rather than copying from me. Perhaps I could help her by showing her which books and websites I found most useful when I was doing my research for the project. Tomorrow I'll find Laura and tell her my reasons for not just handing over my project and why I feel the way I do."

THE NEXT DAY...

"I'm so glad I decided to talk to Laura. I explained to her that I liked the earrings very much but I felt uncomfortable because I wasn't sure about why she had given me the gift – it seemed there may have been an 'ulterior motive' (to make me feel I should loan her my history project). I asked her to put herself in my shoes and imagine how she would feel if I'd done the same thing to her. I expected her to get angry and to try to defend herself, but she said she was really sorry and she wouldn't do it again.

Laura said she appreciated my honesty. She was also glad I hadn't given her an easy way out because she would have felt bad about handing something in that wasn't truly her own work. I reassured her that she is more than capable of doing the project herself, and I promised that I'd help her find the books and webpages I'd used so that she could work on the project over the weekend.

In the end, I didn't send Laura the thank-you letter. I had, after all, thanked her at the time. As it turned out, I was the one to receive a card from Laura! I was touched by what she wrote in it. She said sometimes true friends challenge us to become better people and she thanked me for being honest with her and telling her the truth."

GLOSSARY

Appreciation – A feeling of thanks or gladness about something

Benefactor – A person who gives time, attention, money or other goods

Beneficiary – A person who receives a gift or other kind of benefit

Benefit – Something that does someone good or gives them an advantage

Intention – A clear plan to behave or act in a certain way

Mixed emotions – Feeling a mixture of things about something. For example, a person could feel both happy and sad about something at the same time

Motivation – A reason (or reasons) for acting or behaving in a particular way

Motives – The reasons that explain the way a person acts

Ulterior motive – A reason for behaving or acting in a way that is not immediately apparent or openly admitted

NOTES FOR PARENTS, GUARDIANS, TEACHERS AND FACILITATORS

In this story, Maya reflects on her experience and understanding of gratitude. Over the course of the narrative she talks about different kinds of gratitude, things that impact on a person's experience of gratitude, and the different ways people can demonstrate their thankfulness to others. The story begins with a relatively uncomplicated example of Maya's gratitude to her mum, step-father and siblings for a bicycle and helmet she received for her most recent birthday. Maya's gratitude complements her family's generosity in giving the gift. This uncomplicated experience of gratitude is characterised by positive feelings; she tells us that 'everyone felt good'.

As the story develops, however, Maya begins to explore the topic of gratitude more deeply, bringing up a number of factors that affect the way gratitude is experienced. Maya's story has been written to stimulate discussion about gratitude in the classroom and at home, giving young people an opportunity to reflect on the complexities of this everyday social emotion and valued strength of character.

KEY LEARNING POINTS

- *It is appropriate to be grateful for gifts that are well-intentioned:* Maya recognises her Nani's kind *intentions* in giving her the pink scarf for her birthday, even though it isn't *exactly* to her taste. Maya comments that the importance of a benefactor's intentions might be something younger children (like her sister) would not be able to understand, highlighting the developmental aspects of gratitude.

- *It is appropriate to be grateful for non-realised benefits (benefits that ultimately fail to materialise):* Maya was grateful for the nomination she received for her rendition of the song from *Oliver*, even though she didn't win the "big prize". These first two learning points both exemplify the adage that "It's the thought that counts".

- *There are different types of gratitude:* Maya tells us that some types of gratitude are expressions of politeness (such as thanking someone for holding open a door for us or thanking the driver when we step off the bus). But Maya reflects on the fact that gratitude isn't *just* a question of politeness; we don't mean "thank you" in the same way when someone holds a door open as we do when someone saves a life.

- *Gratitude links us to other people and builds social bonds:* Maya recognises that when we are grateful we acknowledge the steps other people have taken to benefit us. This "makes people feel valued". It also helps us to recognise that we are not the sole authors of our enjoyment and accomplishments in life; for instance, we depend on a lot of other people in order to enjoy a pizza for our dinner, or to learn how to read.

- *We can show gratitude in different ways:* Feeling grateful is just a part of gratitude. In order to show our gratitude to others we can say thank you, write a thank-you letter or card, and reciprocate kindness where we can.

- *It is appropriate to be grateful when people are fulfilling the requirements of their job:* Maya's family were hugely grateful to the surgeon who said she was "just doing her job" when she carried out Arun's appendectomy. We can be grateful to people who look after us; it might well be our parents' and guardians' job to do that, but that doesn't mean there's no need for us to be grateful because it's a part of the "job description"!

- *Our gratitude is boosted when people make an effort to benefit us:* Maya was especially grateful to the friend who went above and beyond what she expected when he helped her learn her lines for drama club.

- *People sometimes have ulterior motives for giving us gifts or doing us a favour:* Maya reports on her mixed feelings when she comes to suspect that a friend has given her a gift to manipulate her. She reflects on the fact that the *reasons* people give us gifts are important – perhaps even more than the gifts themselves.

- *We can sometimes become grateful over time, especially for difficult experiences:* Maya tells us that we can be grateful for what we learn from our mistakes, though we may not feel that way at the time!

ITEMS FOR GROUP DISCUSSION

1   Share your most recent experience of gratitude with the group.

2   Does the intention to benefit someone always matter more than the benefit itself?

3   How do we know that other people mean the same thing by gratitude as we mean ourselves?

4   Do people in different countries have the same understanding of gratitude?

5   Explain the difference between saying thank you out of habit and saying thank you when you really mean it.

6   Can you think of creative ways to show gratitude to others?

7   Can you think of an experience in your life that was difficult at the time but you are now grateful for?

RECOMMENDED READING, RESOURCES AND ORGANISATIONS

TEACHING RESOURCES

www.jubileecentre.ac.uk/userfiles/jubileecentre/
pdf/character-education/GratitudeAndCompassion/
GrowingGratitudeTeacherHandbook.pdf

www.jubileecentre.ac.uk/userfiles/jubileecentre/
pdf/character-education/GratitudeAndCompassion/
GrowingGratitudeStudentWorkbook.pdf

JOURNAL ARTICLES AND BOOK CHAPTERS

Carr, D., Morgan, B. and Gulliford, L. (2015)
"Learning and teaching virtuous gratitude." *Oxford Review of Education*, 41 (6), 766–781.

Gulliford, L. and Morgan, B. (2016) "An Empirical Exploration of the Normative Dimensions of Gratitude." In D. Carr (ed.) *Gratitude: An Interdisciplinary Approach*. London: Routledge.

Gulliford, L. and Morgan, B. (2016) *Taking thanks for granted: Unravelling the concept of gratitude in a developmental cross-cultural analysis*. Report for the Society for Educational Studies (SES).

Gulliford, L. and Morgan, B. (2017) "The Meaning and Valence of Gratitude in Positive Psychology." In N.J.L. Brown, T. Lomas and F.J. Eiroa Orosa (eds) *Critical Positive Psychology*. London: Routledge.

Gulliford, L., Morgan, B. and Kristjánsson, K. (2013) "Recent work on the concept of gratitude in philosophy and psychology." *Journal of Value Inquiry*, 47 (3), 285–377.

Morgan, B., Gulliford, L. and Kristjánsson, K. (2014) "Gratitude in the UK: A new prototype analysis and a cross-cultural comparison." *Journal of Positive Psychology,* 9 (4), 291–294.

Morgan, B. and Gulliford, L. (2017) "Assessing Influences on Gratitude Experience: Age-Related Differences in How Gratitude is Understood and Experienced." In J. Tudge and L. Frietas (eds) *Developing Gratitude in Children and Adolescents.* Cambridge: Cambridge University Press.

Morgan, B., Gulliford, L. and Carr, D. (2015) "Educating gratitude: Some conceptual and moral misgivings." *Journal of Moral Education*, 44 (1), 97–111.